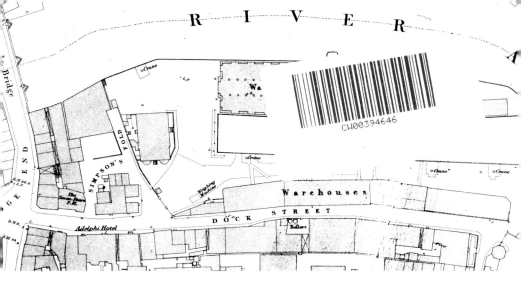

" LEEDS UPON AIRE "

The tiny hamlet of "Loidis in Elmete" was founded on the North Bank of the River Aire well over a thousand years ago, probably on the line of the Roman Road between Chester and York. Its geographical location was ideal, with the river navigable eastwards to the Humber and North Sea. Its hinterland was rich in produce such as wool, skins, grain and root crops.

The Aire continued to serve Leeds, one of the great "boom" towns of the 19th century Industrial Revolution, with its ever-growing commercial role. Indeed the river became even more important when the canal linking the city with Liverpool was completed early in the 19th century. This route, which linked the North and Irish Seas, soon found it had a strong competitor in the form of the "new" railway. From this time the Waterways began to decline as a means of carrying goods.

Leeds Bridge

The river has not been treated kindly during the last century or so, in fact it has been abused. The growth of industry (and population) in West Yorkshire led to its polluted state, though steps are being taken to improve its condition.

*L*eeds has tended to "turn its back" on the river, particularly in the city centre. The railway builders constructed their tracks on the high viaduct which forms such a strong physical and visual barrier between the busy shopping streets and the Aire. Though these are little more than a hundred yards apart, some citizens are quite unaware of the presence of the River and Canal and this is one reason why the Leeds Civic Trust has published this guide.

The past decade has seen a dramatic transformation in the fortunes of Leeds Waterfront. Much neglect and decay has given way to attractive environments in which new buildings have been introduced to blend with carefully conserved warehouses. There is now a resident population numbered in hundreds and you can enjoy a pint in one of the waterside pubs. Life has returned to the waterfront and although the cranes are now idle you can still find many traces of former industrial activity side by side with brand new apartments.

The Trust is committed to a policy that calls for the rejuvenation of the Leeds waterways by a careful balance of conservation and new development that will foster the return of a working and residential community, the cleaning of the river and encouragement for those who would use it for recreational and commercial purposes.

After all, why should the city not bear the title "Leeds-Upon-Aire"?

LOUIS LE PRINCE
Louis Aimé August Le Prince came to Leeds in 1866 where he experimented in cinematography. In 1888 he patented a one-lens camera with which he filmed Leeds Bridge from this British Waterways building. These were probably the world's first successful moving pictures.

1 *COMMENCE ON LEEDS BRIDGE (BRIDGE END)* the original river crossing on the east side, looking downstream. The bridge was built in 1873, replacing an original medieval structure which was the site of the famous Leeds Cloth Market. Note the wall plaques on your right relating to the Band of Hope and to the first moving pictures ever made, by Louis le Prince (1888).

From the bridge there is an excellent view of the Calls/Riverside area. On your immediate right *the former Simpsons Fold* Warehouses, mid 19th century and listed. Beyond these the Victoria Quays development (later description). On the north side, to your left, a new housing complex whose stone base storey and arches formerly supported a massive warehouse, regrettably destroyed by fire in the 60's. Beyond this a group of former warehouse buildings terminating with the tower of Leeds Parish Church.

THE WALK

Cross Leeds Bridge and turn left into Dock Street.

2 At the junction of Hunslet Road and Dock Street you will see the **British Waterways Board's Dock Street offices** opposite the **Adelphi, a Tetley's Heritage pub**, which has a wealth of Victorian craftsmanship in timber and glass.

Take the first left into Navigation Walk, the Victoria Quays housing development.

3 You are now on the site of the *former Aire and Calder Navigation Warehouses and Terminus* (1815 to 1821) where a mixture of converted warehouses and new dwellings was built giving a total of *120 units (1985-1988 by Barratts)*. Substantial support by an urban development grant enabled the project to get under way. This was the first major private housing scheme on the Leeds Waterfront. It is interesting to look at the buildings in detail to differentiate old and new parts. The spaces between buildings are treated attractively with large areas of traditional stone setts.

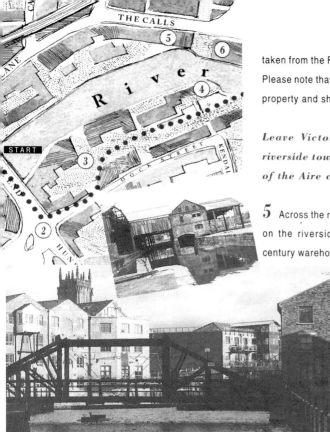

taken from the Flax Warehouse after its conversion. Please note that the area across the bridge is private property and should not be entered.

Leave Victoria Quays - proceed to the riverside towpath, where the opposite side of the Aire can be viewed.

5 Across the river, to your left, is the tallest building on the riverside, a substantial listed early 19th century warehouse *(32 The Calls)*. This is now mainly residential with an attractive waterfront bar and restaurant at lower level *(Sparrows Wharf)*. This has an attractive interior with its original brick vaults, leading onto a waterside terrace.

Proceed through the dwellings keeping to the right hand (south) side of the internal dock.

4 This dock is now relatively shallow. It is planted with lilies and fountains aerate the water intermittently. However, when the canal depot existed this was a deep dock in which barges were moored and unloaded beneath a huge roof, which was removed in 1985. Across the dock is *the original flyboat warehouse with its arched opening at water level*. The timber footbridge across the dock was created by the use of two roof trusses

Sparrows Wharf

6   Also across the river four former derelict warehouses have been converted into a *39 bed hotel and restaurant* by "A Way of Life" (1991). Popular with business users, this hotel, *"42 The Calls"*, offers riverside conference facilities with state-of-the-art communications equipment. Note the contrast of the old buildings with the modern high-tech cable structure carrying the river terrace balcony.

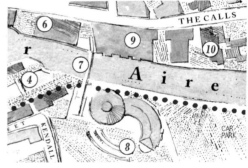

7   Adjacent to the hotel, *the new Centenary footbridge*, the first bridge across the Aire in central Leeds for over 100 years (1992). Designed by Ove Arup this single span suspension bridge has a single support tower on the south bank. The bridge has been instrumental in opening up the south bank of the river, giving access for residents, workers and visitors to Tetley's Brewery Wharf and the Royal Armouries.

Proceed along the towpath and under the footbridge. Pause to view buildings on both sides of the river.

8   On the south bank of the river adjacent to the Centenary footbridge is *Brewery Wharf (1993/94)*. Developed by *Joshua Tetley & Son*, who have been associated with the city for many years, the site of a former cleansing depot has been transformed into a *major leisure, tourist and visitor attraction*. Brewery Wharf introduces you to the fascinating history of the English pub, from the 14th century alehouse through the Elizabethan, Georgian and Victorian periods to a public house of the future, all complete with "period" actors. The Keels Restaurant has a waterfront terrace and a family attraction is the home of the Tetley Shire horses. Traditional skills and crafts linked with pubs and brewing are demonstrated. Recently opened, it is anticipated that Brewery Wharf will attract 250,000 visitors annually.

9 Opposite and immediately across the Aire is *No 46 The Calls*, the conversion of a 1930's brick warehouse into the *Design and Innovation Centre* (1988), offices and studios for architects and designers. The three distinctive towers replaced industrial loading bays and all the balconies are new additions. A good example of how modern design can be used in the conversion of older buildings.

Walk along the towpath towards Crown Point Bridge.

10 Across the river and adjacent to the Design and Innovation Centre is *Langton's Wharf* (1992), 48-52 The Calls.

This residential development has 67 flats with basement car parking. Note how the layout allows for *a view of the Parish Church Tower* through an internal courtyard. The name Langton's derives from the former owners of the site, which was a builders merchants' yard. The Langton brothers were more famous, however, for their exploits in the Isle of Man TT races between the world wars.

Langton's Wharf

11 To the right of the newly built Langton's Wharf its neighbour *The Chandlers* is an interesting blend of old and new. The existing buildings were built in 1876 as a corn chandlers by William Turton, who engaged in supplying food for horses and also ran the Leeds horse trams. The scheme (1987) was built under Housing Association auspices but about half of the flats have now been sold.

12 The Chandlers abuts the listed *Crown Point Bridge*, built in 1840 as a toll bridge. The bridge has a fine iron fretted facade and was widened and repaired in 1994, a very complex engineering exercise.

The route along the towpath under the bridge is likely to be affected by engineering operations during this time and footpath closures will be necessary. If access under the bridge is not possible please refer to page 24

If access under the bridge is not possible please refer to page 24

If access is available under the bridge - Proceed under the bridge (or its abutment) and emerge on its eastern side. Walk up to Clarence Road.

THE CALLS

6
9
10
11

CAR
PARK

EAST STREET

CROWN POINT ROAD

Aire

15

7

8

KENDALL STREET

CAR
PARK

12 CROWN POINT
BRIDGE

13
LEEDS DAM WEIR

BOWMAN LANE

CLARENCE ROAD

CROWN POINT ROAD

BULL STREET

14

ROYAL ARMOURI
MUSEUM SITE

Leeds Lock

Goole
Wakefield
Calder &
Hebble

Weir

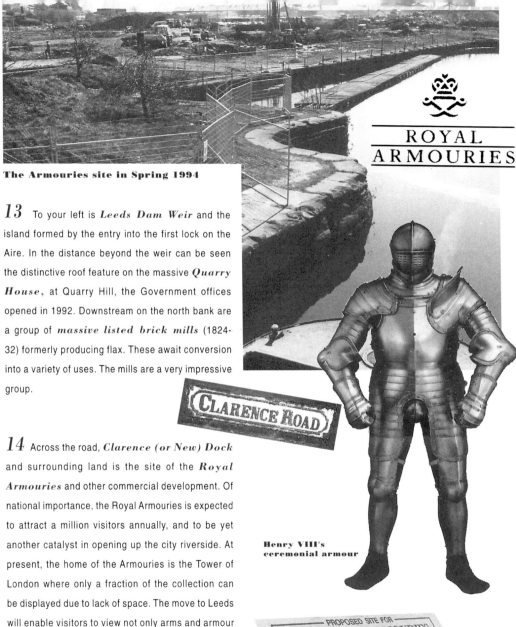

The Armouries site in Spring 1994

13 To your left is **Leeds Dam Weir** and the island formed by the entry into the first lock on the Aire. In the distance beyond the weir can be seen the distinctive roof feature on the massive **Quarry House**, at Quarry Hill, the Government offices opened in 1992. Downstream on the north bank are a group of **massive listed brick mills** (1824-32) formerly producing flax. These await conversion into a variety of uses. The mills are a very impressive group.

CLARENCE ROAD

14 Across the road, **Clarence (or New) Dock** and surrounding land is the site of the **Royal Armouries** and other commercial development. Of national importance, the Royal Armouries is expected to attract a million visitors annually, and to be yet another catalyst in opening up the city riverside. At present, the home of the Armouries is the Tower of London where only a fraction of the collection can be displayed due to lack of space. The move to Leeds will enable visitors to view not only arms and armour from the world's oldest and most prestigious collection but to experience famous battles such as Agincourt or Waterloo through state - of - the art display techniques (opening in Spring 1996).

Henry VIII's ceremonial armour

PROPOSED SITE FOR
THE ROYAL ARMOURIES
MUSEUM
SPONSORED BY
THE LEEDS INITIATIVE AND
THE DEPARTMENT OF THE ENVIRONMENT

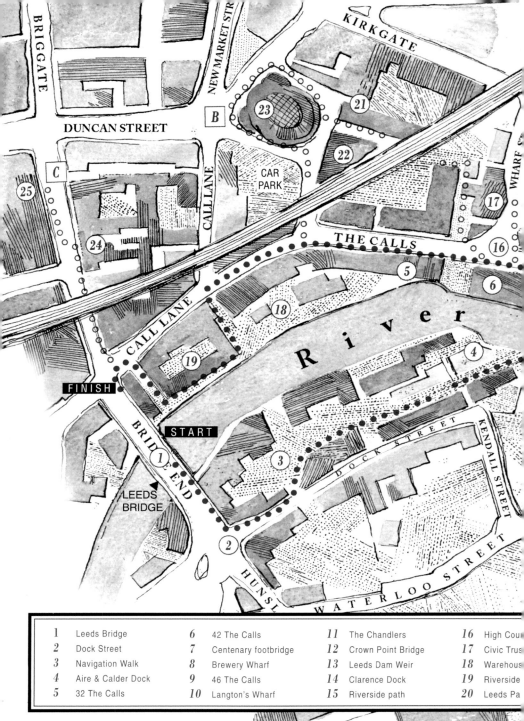

1	Leeds Bridge	6	42 The Calls	11	The Chandlers	16	High Cou
2	Dock Street	7	Centenary footbridge	12	Crown Point Bridge	17	Civic Trus
3	Navigation Walk	8	Brewery Wharf	13	Leeds Dam Weir	18	Warehous
4	Aire & Calder Dock	9	46 The Calls	14	Clarence Dock	19	Riverside
5	32 The Calls	10	Langton's Wharf	15	Riverside path	20	Leeds Pa

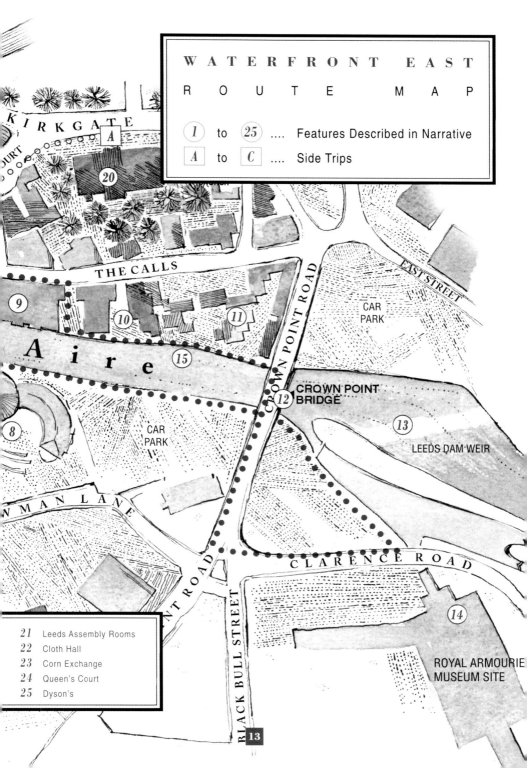

WATERFRONT EAST
R O U T E   M A P

(1) to (25) .... Features Described in Narrative

[A] to [C] .... Side Trips

KIRKGATE

[A]

(20)

THE CALLS

(9)

(10)

(11)

(15)

A i r e

(8)

CAR PARK

WMAN LANE

CROWN POINT ROAD

(12) CROWN POINT BRIDGE

CAR PARK

EAST STREET

(13)

LEEDS DAM WEIR

CLARENCE ROAD

BLACK BULL STREET

ROAD

(14)

ROYAL ARMOURIE MUSEUM SITE

21 Leeds Assembly Rooms
22 Cloth Hall
23 Corn Exchange
24 Queen's Court
25 Dyson's

Turn right and walk along Clarence Road, cross Crown Point Road (take great care). Turn right and cross the bridge over the river, then immediately left down the steps to the riverside path, where you turn right.

15 You are now standing in front of The Chandlers housing. Taking care, proceed along the attractive riverside path with impressive views looking upstream. Turn right at the end of the riverside path and go under the archway "Langtons Wharf", after emerging into The Calls bear left.

The Calls is one of the oldest streets in the city and it has recently been repaired in a traditional way with stone flags and setts which enhance the settings of both refurbished and new developments.

Turn left by No 42 onto Centenary footbridge.

Good views can be enjoyed from the bridge in all directions, enabling you to get a different view of places already visited, and those to come.

Return to the Calls bearing left. Pause at the junction with High Court.

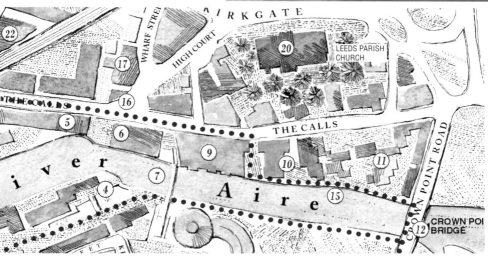

16 This is an important junction in the historic development of the city. On your right the *Old Brewery*, with its decorative brickwork, was converted into offices in 1989. To your left, across the road, *Chancellor Court* is new office development (1990). To its right is a new public walkway leading through the viaduct arch to the Corn Exchange (shops and refreshments). The Corn Exchange, with the adjacent White Cloth Hall, and Assembly Rooms, is well worth a short diversion from your route if you have time. (Notes on these can be found on page 20).

17 Directly, across the road, 11-19 Wharf Street is the conversion of warehouse and cottage into offices, the Shears Yard Restaurant, and at *17-19, the Leeds Civic Trust Heritage & Design Centre*. An interesting diversion from your route would be to visit the latter and *Leeds Parish Church*, only 250 yards away. To get there proceed along High Court, with the Old Brewery to your right (notes on the church can be found on page 19).

Proceed along the Calls westwards, passing (or calling in!) the Sparrows Wharf pub and more warehouses on your left. When you get to the junction of the Calls and Call Lane, turn left down Riverside Court.

18 This area was known as *Warehouse Hill* and once throbbed with commercial activity at its wharves. This location offers excellent views downstream and also of Leeds Bridge to your right. Across the river is *Victoria Quays*, the large converted flax warehouse being most prominent.

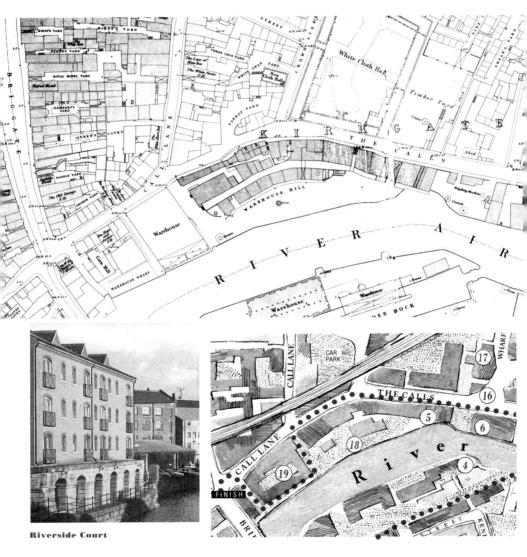

Riverside Court

19   On your right is the *residential development by Tay* located on the site of the old warehouse, whose stone arches still front the riverside with new flats built above. Note the blue Leeds Civic Trust plaque on the stonework describing the Aire and Calder Navigation, opened in 1700. (The Trust has now installed over 30 of these plaques commemorating important people and places around the city).

Leave Warehouse Hill by walking on the riverside path in front of the flats on your right. Turn right up Pitfall Street and left into Call Lane, then immediately left onto Bridge End, and back onto Leeds Bridge.

Historic Briggate, one of the earliest streets in Leeds runs north from Leeds Bridge. There are interesting diversions to view nearby *Queens Court and Dyson's,* the former jewellers and clocksmiths shop (notes on these can be found at the end of this guide).

AIRE AND CALDER NAVIGATION

Before the railway age, the making navigable of the River Aire importantly made Leeds an inland port connected directly to Hull. Cheap water carriage was vital for the successful export of the cloth marketed and finished in the town. Opened 1700

You are now back where you began the walk. Another guided tour booklet covers the interesting river and canal area west of Leeds Bridge. *Why not get a copy and see for yourself!*

17 *Leeds Civic Trust Heritage & Design Centre*

Leeds Civic Trust opened the centre in 1993. The centre provides offices, meeting rooms and exhibition space for the developing activities of the Trust. There is also an information centre and well stocked bookshop specialising in local history, architectural and environmental titles. An old building that has formerly housed a sail and canvas manufacturer and dining rooms continues to serve the community in quite a different way (the centre is normally open weekday mornings and occasional weekend afternoons, but please check first by ringing (0532-439594).

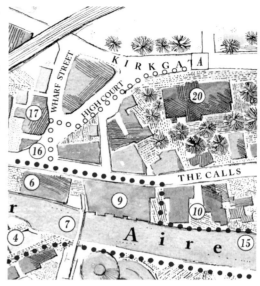

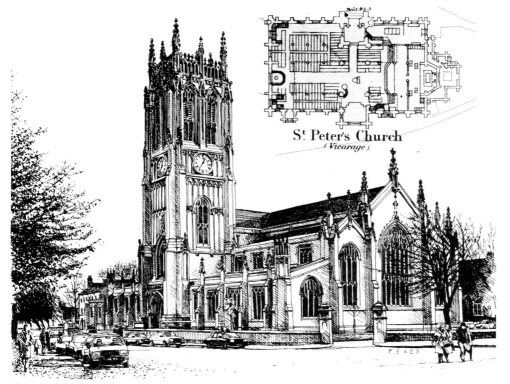

St. Peter's Church
(Vicarage)

20 *Leeds Parish Church*

The present building is relatively new having been built in 1841 to designs by R D Chantrell but it is probable that there was a church here in the 7th century. Seating about 2000 people, its tower is 140 feet high and dominates its local environment. It serves as an important centre for major events in the spiritual life of the city. There are many interior features, a number of which illustrate the history of Leeds. Of particular historic interest is the Anglian style Leeds Cross (10th Century) with both Christian and mythological motifs. The City of Leeds Room is an attractive visitor centre with publications, souvenirs and recordings on sale. Midday refreshments are normally available on weekdays.

The Assembly Rooms (1777), Third White Cloth Hall (1776) and Corn Exchange (1862)

This group of historic buildings is only a few yards from the riverside and is well worth a visit.

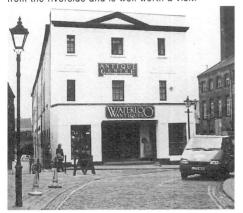

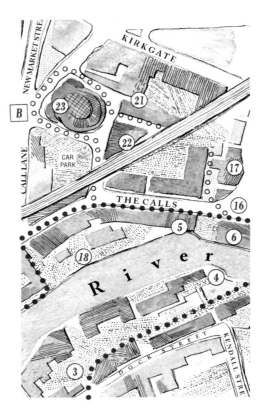

21 *The Leeds Assembly Rooms (Waterloo House)* formed the north wing of the Cloth Hall courtyard and were the social meeting place of the city in Georgian times for around 50 years, with grand ballroom, supper and card rooms. This elegance was to change however when the railway viaduct was built, and after being used as the first working men's institution in Leeds (1868) the building became the home of various tradesmen and commercial enterprises, suffering considerable alteration. Today there are moves to carry out restoration works and the Waterlooo Antiques Centre has many interesting stalls. The small Museum of Georgian Leeds upstairs provides the opportunity to see the original fine plaster ceiling of the former ballroom.

22 What you can see today of the *Cloth Hall* is only a small fragment of the original which had buildings surrounding a huge open courtyard. The railway viaduct was cut through the buildings in the 1860's, leaving only the west block. This cloth market was one of the wonders of commerce in Georgian times. The courtyard was also used for public gatherings and military parades. Today, the remaining building is now used for retail purposes after an attractive conversion.

23 *The Corn Exchange* is a magnificent structure with the external walls giving it an air of great strength and solidity. However, when entering via the west porch the huge, brightly lit interior is revealed as a great surprise, the elegant geometry of the roof framework being likened by many to that of a Zeppelin skeleton. The rooflights were needed functionally so that traders could view and handle grain samples in the "best light". Interestingly, trading in grain still goes on every Tuesday afternoon but with limited numbers when compared with a century ago, of course. Look out for the black bench desks and autioneer's rostrum which still furnish the main level. In the 1950's and 60's, grain trading declined and the building was used for a variety of short term uses during which its condition deteriorated. In 1990 the building re-opened after extensive restoration works and is now a lively and colourful place with interesting small shops and basement cafes, the latter being accessed by newly introduced staircases. The large main floor area is used for weekend market stalls for crafts, antiques and the like. There is a wonderful atmosphere here on a busy weekend, an excellent example of how such old buildings can be given an extended life by introducing new uses.

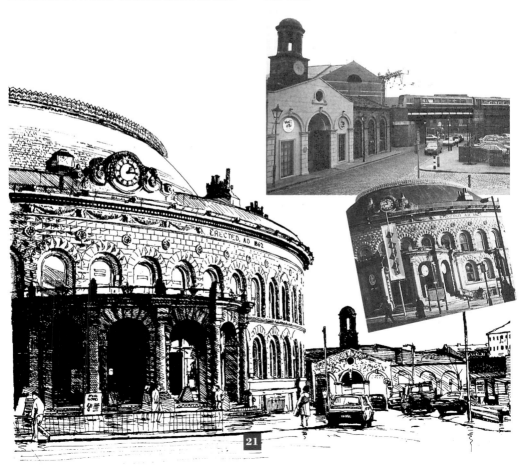

Two places of particular historic interest are located only a short walk up Briggate from Leeds Bridge.

24 *Queen's Court* is typical of the original burgage plots that were laid out on both sides of Briggate in the 13th century (there are several more you can see if you walk further up Briggate). This one is particularly notable because it contains the house, workshop and warehouse of a Leeds wool and cloth merchant during Queen Anne's reign. After suffering much change during the past 200 years with fire and dilapidation, the Court was completely restored in the 1980's. That such yards and courts still exist in the centre of a modern city like Leeds is very important in our appreciation of our urban history and it is very pleasing that several others have been refurbished (or are promised such). Why not have a look by walking up Briggate?

QUEEN'S COUR
This historic courtyard oc
one of the 60 burgage
which abutted Briggate
Middle Ages. It is fronte
eight-bayed woollen
merchant's house (built
and contains the merc
cloth finishing sh
and warehouse

25 The former *Dyson's Jeweller's Shop* is on the west side of Briggate near the Boar Lane junction. No longer trading as such, the building is now a restaurant with its structure and facade preserved in all its glory. Of mid-19th century origin Dyson's has a very elaborate and highly decorative frontage displaying the clocks which also become part of the social life in Leeds, with many citizens arranging to meet their "intended" under these famous time-pieces for "dates". Recently beautifully restored, Dyson's is highly photogenic. The interior is also well worth a visit. Don't miss Dyson's!

DIVERSIONS!

If the route under Crown Point Bridge is closed please refer to this page, notes and sketch map.

There are two options for diversions:-

1 Return along the towpath and cross over the footbridge, rejoining the walk at point 16 (page 15) in the Calls. Note the side trips available to you from this point.

2 If you wish to view the Royal Armouries site proceed as follows. Return along the towpath turning left around the Brewery Wharf into Bowman Lane. When you reach Crown Point Road cross the road (using very great care) via central refuge and into Clarence Road. (See point 14 page 11).

To return, either retrace your steps to Brewery Wharf and Centenary Bridge or proceed as follows.

Cross over Crown Point Bridge using the only footpath that will be open. If this path is on the east side (Armouries side) cross over near the roundabout approach and turn into the Calls. Take very great care at this crossing and observe all highway signs that are in place at the time. Rejoin the walk at point 16 (page 15).

If the path on the west side is open, cross Crown Point Road and bear right over the bridge. You will then be able to rejoin the riverside path at point 15 (page 14), by taking the steps down to the quayside at the bridge end.

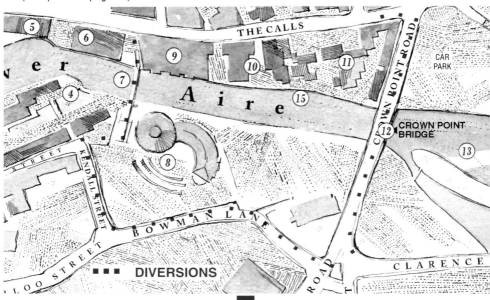

Living World

Simon Oxley

NCEC

NATIONAL CHRISTIAN EDUCATION COUNCIL

Other worship resources published by NCEC

Celebrating Series . . .
A series of six books for all-age festival services:
Celebrating Christmas Books 1 & 2
Celebrating Lent & Easter Books 1 & 2
Celebrating Harvest
Celebrating Special Sundays

Anthologies of material for private reflection and public worship
A Word in Season
Liturgy of Life
Prayers for the Church Community

Cover design: Julian Smith
Cover photo: Methodist Church Overseas Division

Published by:
National Christian Education Council
Robert Denholm House
Nutfield
Redhill, RH1 4HW

British Library Cataloguing-in-Publication Data:
Oxley, Simon
    Living World – (Living Worship Series)
    I. Title II. Series
    264

ISBN 0-7197-0806-0

First published 1993
© 1993 Simon Oxley

Typeset by Avonset, Midsomer Norton, Bath
Printed in Great Britain by
Clifford Frost Ltd, Wimbledon, London

CONTENTS

FOREWORD TO THE SERIES

This is the second in a series of six books which offer services of worship for all ages in the church. The details of the other five can be found on the back cover of the book. The authors write from a wide experience of leading all-age worship and the *Living Worship series* . . . springs from that experience.

In the celebration of Christian worship every age-group has something to contribute. The experiences of each member of the congregation, regardless of age, can be used, and should be valued. The ability and willingness of children to enter into a wide range of worship experiences should not be under-estimated. Adults should be encouraged to accept the gifts which children bring to worship.

There is no 'audience' in all-age worship. The children are not performing for the adults; neither are they passive spectators to adult worship. These services provide the means by which the whole church family can engage in its most important responsibility and joy: the worship of God through Jesus Christ.

These books will serve churches best when a group of people, representative of all ages in the church meet to plan the worship, and are prepared to give time and thought to the preparation. Those who use them should feel free to adapt them to the needs of the local church community. In any one church they may well emerge on a Sunday morning looking quite different from the details given on the printed pages that follow.

Unless the flow of the service requires it, no place is given for either the Lord's Prayer, the offertory, or announcements. These should be included according to local practice.

Series Editor: Donald Hilton

PREFACE

Christians sometimes give the impression that worship is an escape from the world. However, no act of worship can ignore the world; it is where we live our lives, and where we are called to serve God. The world has its origins and its end in God. To fail to taking the world seriously in any act of worship is to fail in being true to who we are, and who God is. Each of these services seek to concentrate our worship on a specific aspect of the world's life.

Harvest Festivals have planted themselves firmly in the Church's calendar and in the expectations of many congregations; *Thankful Hearts* offers a way of using the opportunity to reflect on the gifts we have been given and receive. One World Week and the Week of Prayer for World Peace have not established themselves so firmly but nonetheless present us with themes which lie at the heart of our faith. To our shame, Christians are often seen to be people who put up barriers between each other, both inside and outside the church. *Don't Build Walls* challenges in worship our wall-building tendencies.

Many worship leaders, particularly those who have had no personal experience of world wars, find Remembrance Sunday worship difficult to plan yet some in our congregations have a pastoral need 'to remember' in worship. Yet others would prefer not to observe the day, or want to use it in a different way. *True Memorials* offers one way into worship for that Sunday.

Scales of Justice is not specific to any time of year and helps us to celebrate God's justice which is so often different from our own.

Simon Oxley

THANKFUL HEARTS
A service for harvest thanksgiving

Introduction

This is a service of thanksgiving using the harvest as its inspiration. Its aim is to help the congregation to respond in gratitude for all the gifts that God has given, and also for our ability to give. It includes the traditional harvest gifts but is not limited to them.

Preparation

Ask members of the congregation to bring objects or symbols of gifts we have all been given e.g. food, homes, skills, faith, each other, money, the arts etc. and also the gifts we have to share. Prime some individuals to bring specific and particular things so that there is a good cross-section e.g., an amateur artist might bring a painting; an electrician – wires and sockets; a housewife – cake; or a schoolchild – a piece of craft-work.

Ask three or four people to be prepared to talk about opportunities for giving in the church and community e.g., financial (included in the United Reformed Church's 'Commitment for Life' programme, or the Christian Aid Christmas collection), leadership of worship, pastoral care, community involvement.

Set up two large boards. Label one 'Gifts we have been given', the other 'Gifts we can give'. Place a table in front of each one. Pins or blu-tak will be required. If there is to be a traditional harvest display, it should be close to the board labeled 'Gifts we have been given'.

Provide each member of the congregation with two A5 sized pieces of paper.

ORDER OF SERVICE

Give each member of the congregation the two A5 pieces of paper as they enter church.

Call to Worship

Use the present opportunity to the full. Speak to one another in psalms, hymns and songs; sing and make music from your heart to the Lord; and in the name of our Lord Jesus Christ give thanks every day for everything to God our Father.

Ephesians 5.16a, 19, 20 (REB)

Paul encouraged the Christians at Ephesus to respond to God with thankful hearts. We as Christians in (*name your church or town*) want to thank God today too.

Hymn   'Think of a world without any flowers'   *(471 My God I thank Thee)*

Prayer *M.C*   *We really want thank you Lord.* 234

To the leader's words: Our hearts are full of thankfulness.
Invite the people to respond with: **We praise and worship you.**

Our God, we know you in your creation.
We praise you for the wonder and beauty of your world;
for all that we can see, hear, touch, taste and smell,
for the life that you have given to each one of us.
Our hearts are full of thankfulness.
We praise and worship you.

Our God, we know you in Jesus Christ.
We praise you for your amazing love shown in his living, dying and rising again;
for the story we read in the gospels
for his presence with us now,
our hearts are full of thankfulness.
We praise and worship you.

Our God, we know you in the work of the Holy Spirit.
We praise you for the energy you give us to put our faith into action inside and outside the church;
for the comfort and inspiration you give us.
Our hearts are full of thankfulness.
We praise and worship you. Amen.

Comment – Saying 'Thank You,'

Children are always being told by parents or other adults not to forget to say thank you. When they forget, someone in a loud stage-whisper is bound to ask, 'What do you say?' After a party, or being taken out for a treat or receiving a present, we learn at a very early age that we should say thank you.

It's not just children who are told to say thank you. When staff are trained to work in shops, hotels, restaurants or banks or wherever they have to meet the public, they are reminded how important it is to say thank you.

Our service today affirms the importance of saying thank you to God, as well as to other people.

Hymn   'Thank you, Lord, for this new day'
or other hymn of thanksgiving

[handwritten: or 633 Thank you Jesu | 734. I really want the | 24. All things | Praise thee]

The gifts we have been given.

[handwritten: Margaret / Stuart / Fred / May You God!]

*Ask everyone to take one of their pieces of paper and write or draw on it something (an object, a place, a skill, a person) for which they want to thank God. Invite everyone to stick their pieces of paper on the 'Gifts we have been given' board. Also ask those people who have brought particular objects or pictures with them to church (see **Preparation**) to add these too.*

Draw attention to the wide range of gifts we have been given. If there is a traditional harvest display mention some of the items on the display. Give an opportunity for comment on anything which has been forgotten and add it to the board.

[handwritten: Solo - Elizabeth - Give thanks 170]

Story: *Giving and Receiving*

David Cowling was working with the Methodist Church Overseas Division in Kenya when he learnt an important lesson about receiving gifts thankfully. This is what he wrote:

'When you are 150 miles from home with only a small car and you are visiting a village for the first time, you don't expect to be given a sheep. In any case, I was no longer living on a farm and a suburban garden has limited possibilities for accommodating sheep.

My home was in Nairobi, Kenya and I was visiting a village with Arnold who works as a farm advisor for the Catholic Diocese of Machakos. We had visited farms in the village but I was told that we were now to be presented with a sheep. I protested that I did not need a sheep but Arnold explained that it would offend our hosts if I did not accept. I reluctantly agreed and said I would then try to send a selection of farm tools to the village when I returned to Nairobi. Arnold responded angrily that I was making the typical response of a white, English expatriate. "Why can't you just receive something?"

he asked, "Why do you always have to be the one giving?" '

In telling the story, David Cowling adds a prayer which we will pray together now.

read now

Prayer

Joan ?

Yes, Lord, why do I always want to give?
Am I too proud to receive,
    too busy to receive,
    too blind to receive?
Show me how much I can learn from others
    how my life makes more sense when there is time for others
    how in receiving from others I can receive from you.

Jonathan Kerry

Hymn   'For the beauty of the earth'

152. For the Beauty of the Earth.

POEM

The gifts we can give

Ask everyone to write or draw on the other piece of paper what they think they or the church can give to others. Invite everyone to stick their piece of paper on the 'Gifts we can give' board. Also invite three or four people (see **Preparation***) to talk very briefly about the opportunities for giving or using gifts that exist in the church.*

Look at the match between the gifts we have been given and the gifts we need to share. Are there gifts we have been given which we have yet to learn to use?

Prayer of Thanksgiving

Penny ? or Joan

Use the following as a basis, adapting it to include items featured in the two displays. Invite the congregation to sing the refrain of the hymn, 'We plough the fields and scatter' after each section of the thanksgiving.

Father we thank you for all your gifts to us:
    for food . . .
    for homes, families, friends . . .
    for everything which makes life enjoyable and
        interesting . . .
        All good gifts around us
        are sent from heaven above;
        then thank the Lord, O thank the Lord,
        for all his love.

for physical skills . . .
for artistic gifts . . .
for gifts of caring . . .
> **All good gifts around us . . .**

for the church, its worship, its fellowship . . .
for the call to follow and live the Christian life . . .
for the resources of faith . . .
> **All good gifts around us . . .**

for the love of God experienced in Jesus . . .
for hope . . .
for joy . . .
> **All good gifts around us . . .**

LORDS PRAYER

Hymn 'For the fruits of his creation.' *24 All things*
or other harvest hymn. *Praise thee*

Reading 2 Corinthians 9.6-15 *— Mum / Joan*

Reflection on the Bible passage
Who gives us presents? Think about birthdays, Christmas, anniversaries etc. Presents come from a variety of people. God is the greatest giver. All that is good in life comes from God.

How do we thank God? Not only by saying 'thank you' but also by being generous to those who need to receive our gifts. *II*

Who benefits from this giving and receiving? Both those who receive and those who give. Giving doesn't deprive the givers, it benefits them. *V*

Prayer of Intercession *— George / Ailsa*
Let us pray for those who are prevented from enjoying all God's gifts, and for ourselves.
To the leader's words: May those who sow in tears.
invite the response: **Reap with shouts of joy.**

> O God our creator,
> whose good earth is entrusted
> to our care and delight and tenderness,
> we pray:
> > May those who sow in tears
> > **Reap with shouts of joy.**

11

For all who are in captivity to debt,
whose lives are cramped by fear
from which there is no turning
except through abundant harvest.
>   May those who sow in tears
>   **Reap with shouts of joy.**

For all who depend on the earth
for their daily food and fuel
whose forests are destroyed
for the profits of the few.
>   May those who sow in tears
>   **Reap with shouts of joy.**

For all who labour in poverty,
who are oppressed by unjust laws,
who are banned for speaking the truth,
who long for a harvest of justice.
>   May those who sow in tears
>   **Reap with shouts of joy.**

For all who are in captivity
to greed and waste and boredom,
whose harvest joy is choked
with things they do not need.
>   May those who sow in tears
>   **Reap with shouts of joy.**

Turn us again from our captivity,
and restore our vision,
that our mouth may be filled with laughter
and our tongue with singing. Amen

Janet Morley

Offering

Suggest to the congregation that our offering is both a means and a sign of sharing our gifts. Invite everyone to take what they had put on the displays and lay them on the Communion Table.

Offertory Prayer
Sing a verse from 'We plough the fields and scatter'.
    'We thank you then, O Father,
    for all things bright and good,
    the seed time and the harvest,
    our life, our health, our food.
    No gifts have we to offer
    for all your love imparts,
    but that which you most welcome,
    our humble, thankful hearts.'

Hymn   'Now thank we all our God'

Benediction

DON'T BUILD WALLS
A service for One World Week
or for the Week of Prayer for World Peace

Introduction

The old saying that 'a good fence makes good neighbours' may have some truth in it but if relationships are good, no fence at all can create 'fullness of life' for ourselves and others.

Too readily we hedge ourselves in and deny the contact with others that can make life more fruitful. History is full of walls: the Great Wall of China, Hadrian's Wall, the Berlin Wall. Walls can divide races, nations, and families.

Christ, who 'has broken down the barrier of enmity' (*Ephesians 2.14*) between people and God has been a powerful influence in breaking down all dividing walls, and in discouraging us from building new ones.

This service examines the walls that divide people from people and asks for the help of God in breaking them down.

Preparation

Decorate the church with pictures of dividing walls of any kind. Collect slides of various kinds of walls (go through your own or other people's holiday pictures) to be shown on a projector and screen.

Draw an outline of a building on an acetate and have an overhead projector available to project it. Alternatively, draw a picture large enough for all the congregation to see.

Collect enough cardboard boxes to build part of a wall at the front of the church. Some should be labelled (e.g., family, church, the nation, money, opinions, differences; see details in the **Order of Service**). Stack the boxes at the side of the church ready for when needed.

Where possible use prayers prepared for the current year's One World Week or Week of Prayer for World Peace.

At the service the previous week invite all or some of the congregation to look through local and national newspapers for examples of incidents which show that we live in a divided world.

Encourage them to summarise the incident in a few sentences and then form a single sentence beginning with: 'I wish we could help break down the wall between . . .'

ORDER OF SERVICE

Call to Worship
Use three voices to speak the three sections.
How good and pleasant it is
to live together as brothers in unity!
It is as if the dew of Hermon were falling
on the mountains of Zion.
There the Lord bestows his blessing,
life for evermore.

Psalm 133. 1,   3 (REB)

Christ is himself our peace. Gentiles and Jews, he has made the two one, and in his own body of flesh and blood, has broken down the barrier of enmity which separated them; for he annulled the law with its rules and regulations, so as to create out of the two a single new humanity in himself, thereby making peace.

Ephesians 2.14-15 (REB)

In you, Lord, I have found refuge;
let me never be put to shame.
By your saving power rescue and deliver me;
hear me and save me!
Be to me a rock of refuge
to which at all times I may come;
you have decreed my deliverance,
for you are my rock and stronghold.

Psalm 71.1-3 (REB

Hymn   'A safe stronghold our God is still'
                or 'All my hope on God is founded'

Introduction
One of the psalms at the start of worship and the hymn which we have just sung remind us that God is our protector. He is more reliable than anyone or anything in the world.

15

Prayer

Eternal God, we have learned to trust. In times of trouble we have leaned on family and friends, and found security. When others have leaned on us, we have found joy in being trustworthy. We give thanks for every sign of confidence and trust in our relationship with others.

But sadly we have also learned not to trust. There have been sad times when people have let us down and times when we have failed others.

The world around us seems trustworthy and strong – the regular seasons, the rising dawn, sweeping tides and solid ground.

Yet we have seen natural disaster and disease destroy the lives of people and our confidence in the world and humanity is shaken.

So we turn to you, God. You are solid ground beneath our uncertain feet. You are the friend on whom we can lean. You are husband and wife, mother and father, constant companion. You are the promise of good things to come. Trusting in your strength we find courage enough to face whatever life brings; strength enough to face life and death, trust and loss of trust, and all things. Amen

Why walls?

Explore the idea of walls:
- *show pictures and ask people to guess where the walls are;*
- *or think about the different kinds of walls we experience: those in homes and churches, garden fences, castles, town defences, prisons.*
- *Ask if anyone has visited Hadrian's Wall, the Great Wall of China, or the former Berlin Wall. What impression did the wall create?*
- *Draw on local examples where possible.*

Ask why we build walls:
- *to keep in (people, heat, ideologies etc.),*
- *to keep out (people, cold, wet, wind, alien influences etc.).*

Using the outline of a building drawn on a flip-chart or overhead projector, write up the congregation's suggestions of how and what walls are designed to keep in, or keep out.

Hymn   'In Christ there is no East or West'

What walls?

The hymn reminds us that we are all one in Christ. Yet despite that, we all seem to be wall builders – in nations, churches and as individual people even if our walls are not made of bricks and mortar.

With the help of members of the congregation, start building a wall using the cardboard boxes. As this is done, comment negatively and in your own words on the boxes (bricks) that are labelled. For example:

FAMILY
Families are so important. Let's stay in our own homes and family circles. Keep ourselves to ourselves.

CHURCH
We've got a lovely Christian fellowship in our church. Let's make sure that only the right kind of people join us so that it is not spoiled.

NATION
Pull up the drawbridge. Reject those with foreign passports. We can't let just anyone into our nice country.

WEALTH
Of course we have to help the poor – so long as it doesn't affect our own standard of living.

OPINIONS
Don't confuse me with the facts. I know who I like and who don't like.

DIFFERENCE
I like differences in people. It gives me a chance to show how much better my way of thinking and acting is.

Invite suggestions for labels for other boxes in the wall and write on them.

Hymn   'Kneels at the feet of his friends'
or 'Father of glory whose heavenly plan'

Response
Invite people to read their short summary of incidents culled from newspapers, and share their own one-sentence response.

Break down walls
Introduce and read Ephesians 2.11-22.
Jesus broke down one of the toughest walls – between Jews and gentiles. We should not only opt out of the wall-building business, we should enrol in the wall-breaking business.

Invite people from the congregation to come and break down the cardboard box wall. As the labelled boxes fall comment positively on some of them. For example:

17

FAMILY	But that brick can only be removed if we open our doors and show hospitality to each other and learn to see the world as one family.
CHURCH	That can only go when each church throws its door wide open.
NATION	So just what do we do about refugees?

Story: *Martin Luther King*

Martin Luther King was the minister of a Baptist Church in Montgomery, Alabama in the United States of America. He believed in breaking down walls – the walls white people had built between themselves and black people.

In Montgomery, blacks and whites did not mix. The buses kept the front seats for white people only. If the bus was crowded then black passengers had to give up seats in their part of the bus. One day a black woman called Rosie Parkes refused to give up her seat as more white people got on board. She was arrested. As a protest the local black people agreed not to use the buses.

Martin was elected president of the group organising the protest. A large meeting was held and he was asked to speak to the protestors. "We're here this evening to say to those who have treated us wrong for so long, we're tired. Tired of being kept apart. Tired of being shamed. Tired of being kicked about . . . But we must not be violent. Don't force people not to use the buses. Our actions must be guided by our Christian faith. Remember the words of Jesus: 'Love your enemies. Bless them that curse you. Pray for them that use you badly.' "

Martin Luther King became a leader of a movement across America to give blacks and whites equal rights. Even though the protestors were badly beaten, Martin still called for non-violent protest. Hate had to be defeated by love. He was assassinated in 1968, but his example still encourages people today who are working to break down barriers.

Hymn   'Bind us together, Lord'
        or 'Come all who look to Christ today'

Don't build walls!

Read Zechariah 2.1-5. Introduce the reading by suggesting that Zechariah believed the new Jerusalem would be a city without walls because it must contain many varied people. The only wall it needed was the protection of God. Barrier-building is a sign of the failure of our imagination and shows a lack of trust in God.

Story: *Taizé – a community without walls*

Taizé is a small village in south-eastern France. In that village lives a community of monks who spend their lives in prayer, work and reflection, led by a man called Brother Roger. People come from all over the world and from all Christian traditions, often in large numbers, to spend a week or two with the community. This is what one young person wrote about the experience:

'I found myself spending a week with a thousand or more people from all over Europe and further afield. There was an Australian lad who seemed to have found the place almost by accident, there was a group of young Poles proudly wearing their Solidarity badges; and a lovely girl from Eire who spoke French, German and English as well as Gaelic. There were Dutch people who seemed to speak something of everything, and lots of German people.

The worship was amazing. In the silence a solitary voice sang Alleluia!, and was answered by . . . one hundred?, a thousand?, ten thousand? voices singing Alleluia, Alleluia, Alleluia – it could have been the angels in heaven the sound was so deep and so sweet. The rest of the time we spent in groups which were as international as possible, though with care taken that there was a common language or adequate translation available – and in those groups we lived, worked, discussed and prayed together for the whole week.

At the top of the information sheet we were given on the first day it said "Taizé is a place to search for God and find in Christ a meaning of life". Further down the page it asked us to begin our time at Taizé thinking about this:

> "You are searching for God: you are aware that what matters most is the welcome you extend to Christ the risen Lord. By his presence, always offered to each person, by his forgiveness, he brings you to life. By placing your confidence in him and by forgiving, you will break out of your inner prisons to dare to commit yourself as a pilgrim of reconciliation, even in the divisions of the Christian family and those which tear apart the whole human family."

This is not a super-pious place where religion is far removed from reality. It is a hard place to be because it demands decisions – maybe only little ones – but you come home a different person. It brings you into contact with people you have never met, whose very being challenges your previously held assumptions.'

from an unnamed report

Prayer

Begin with prayer for current situations in the world, the local community and the church. Prayers in material prepared for 'One World Week' or the 'Week of Prayer for World Peace' could be used. Conclude with the following prayer:

To the leader's words: Break down the walls that separate us.
Invite the congregation to respond with the words: **And unite us in a single body.**

Lord, you made the world and gave life to all creatures;
You made all people one people and gave us the earth as our home.
> Break down the walls that separate us.
> **And unite us in a single body.**

Lord, our thoughts, our words and our actions have built barriers;
we have lived behind walls of prejudice and ignorance;
we have been quick to label and classify each other.
> Break down the walls that separate us.
> **And unite us in a single body.**

Lord, you show us that you want us to live in unity with each other, turning our backs on old hatreds and injustices which divide us
and seeking the ways of peace and freedom
> Break down the walls that separate us.
> **And unite us in a single body.**

Lord, help us to know your will,
give us courage to do what is right no matter what opposition we meet.
give us patience to keep on fighting all that is evil or unjust,
and the grace to be actively making friends across all dividing lines.
> Break down the walls that separate us.
> **And unite us in a single body.**
>> Adapted from prayers used at the WCC Nairobi Assembly

Hymn   'Go forth and tell'
               or any other hymn of commitment and mission

Benediction

SCALES OF JUSTICES

Introduction

To call God 'judge' can give a distorted idea of him. It may evoke a picture of a robed figure who dispassionately weighs the evidence and then 'makes the punishment fit the crime'. Whilst the image of the scales of justice may be healthy for legislative justice, it fails to represent the way God deals with us.

Preparation

You will need kitchen and bathroom scales.

Construct a large balance with a broom handle, rope, and tea-trays. Suspend the broom handle from some convenient and secure place or say from a pair of step-ladders bridged with a plank. It will be more secure if the suspended rope is attached to the balance point (centre) of the broom handle. It is essential the rope supporting each tray is an equal distance from the centre of the broom handle.

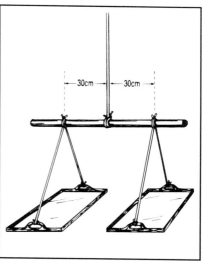

ORDER OF SERVICE

Call to Worship

It is God who will judge the world with justice,
who will try the cause of people with equity.
May the Lord be a tower of strength for the oppressed,
a tower of strength in time of trouble.
Those who acknowledge your name will trust in you,
for you, Lord, do not abandon those who seek you.

Psalm 9.8-10 (REB)

Hymn   'There's a spirit in the air'

Prayer

O God, you have created us to be your people and to live in your freedom.

Your Son, Jesus Christ, has called us to serve you.

Your Holy Spirit has filled us with your life.

We praise you that you are God and Father to each one of us, and without favourites.

We thank you for the rich variety of life and that we find your love in every experience. As we worship may we be open to your spirit of justice so that we can discover how to live with integrity and hope. Amen

Reading   Luke 1.46-55

Introduce the reading as a picture of the 'upside-down' world of Jesus in which those whom life has cast down are raised up.

By coupling verses 46 and 47 as one verse this can be read responsively with either the leader reading the first part of each verse and the congregation responding with the second , or by using two voices, each reading one part of each verse.

Hymn   'Go tell it on the mountain'

Balanced Justice

Introduce the idea of weighing by demonstrating kitchen scales and bathroom scales. Weigh objects on the kitchen scales and people on the bathroom scales. (Be sensitive to those for whom body weight is a problem.)

The simplest weighing machine is the balance. With the assistance of previously selected members of the congregation, make a large balance in the way suggested in the Preparation. Do some experiments e.g., with Bibles and hymn books. Demonstrate that balance is obtained by the weight on one side being equal to the weight on the other.

Comment

That's the way we usually see justice. The evidence is weighed, and guilt or innocence is proved. *If possible show a picture, or transparency – or project an acetate on an overhead projector – of 'justice' as a figure with scales above 'Old Bailey'.*

In the last century, Charles Kingsley wrote a book called *The Water Babies*. It's about the misfortunes of a chimney sweep called Tom. In the days of open fires, chimneys had to be swept regularly. In large houses the chimneys were so large that small boys were sent up the chimney to clean them. In his adventures, Tom meets two characters – Mrs. Bedonebyasyoudid and Mrs. Doasyouwouldbedoneby. Mrs. Doasyouwouldbedoneby was kind and encouraged people to be good to others, just as you hope that other people will be good to you. The other woman, Mrs. Bedonebyasyoudid, was not so kind. She made sure that whatever unkind thing you did to other people happened to you too. But whether it was kind or not, at least it seemed fair. You got what you deserved.

Hymn   'Seek ye first the kingdom of God'

Unfair Justice

Present the following sketch based on Matthew 20.1-16 or use it in advance of the session to stimulate a group to write or improvise a similar sketch of their own.

The five men for hiring should sit or lie in a central area, dozing. There should be an exit through which they go when hired. The only props needed are packets of jelly babies but the play can be enhanced by having a child's clock which the Boss can change to 9, 12, 3 o'clock etc.

Boss	(*He/she walks into central area, looking quite officious and speaks first to A whom he/she tries to waken*) Hello! (*no response*) Hello! (*no response*) Hello, what are you doing?
A	I was sleeping until . . .
Boss	(*Interrupting*) I mean what are you doing for a job . . . work . . . employment?
A	Oh, I'm redundant . . . Nobody wants me.
Boss	Would you like a job?
A	Would I?
Boss	No, I don't have a wood eye, just a bad squint. Would you like a job?
A	Yes.
Boss	Right, then. I want you to spot elephants until six o'clock this evening.
A	What?
Boss	I want you to spot elephants.
A	What colour of spots do you want? Yellow? Blue? Or perhaps you'd like some nice pink ones?

23

Boss	I wouldn't like that at all! I want you to count them … like spotting trains.
A	Are these British Rail elephants, by any chance?
Boss	No, they are not. Just go out the door, into the main street and start spotting. I'll call you back at 6 o'clock.
A	Have you a notebook? I mean you don't know how many there'll be in (*Name your own town or area*) on a day like this.
Boss	Just use your fingers.
A	How much do I get for all this?
Boss	A packet of Smarties . . . No, I'm sorry, they make a mess of your fingers if your hands sweat. I know . . . a packet of jelly babies.
A	I can't wait till 6 o'clock! (*He goes off*)
Boss	(*Turning clock from 6 to 9 and trying to waken B*) Hello, my little golden wonder . . . Would you like tea or coffee?
B	Tea, please, and two slices of toast.
Boss	Who do you think I am?
B	Let me see . . . did you come on a bike?
Boss	Matter of fact, I did.
B	Then you must be Norman Tebbit.
Boss	No, I'm not . . . But I've a job for you if you want it.
B	When do I start?
Boss	Right away.
B	What do I do?
Boss	You spot elephants.
B	What's the pay like?
Boss	A packet of jelly babies at 6 o'clock.
B	Is there a lunch break?
Boss	No.
B	Why not?
Boss	It might put you off your jelly babies.
B	OK, then. (*He moves off, then turns on his heel*) Oh, do you want to know the elephants' names?
Boss	No, just their numbers.
B	See you at six!
Boss	(*Winds clock to 12 and wakens C*) Ding dong, ding dong etc. (*Like 'Big Ben'*)
C	It's the News at Ten . . . I must have slept for ages!
Boss	No, its not the ten o'clock news. Its twelve midday and I want to offer you a job.

C	You must be Santa Claus!
Boss	No, its just after Pentecost (*Or some other time as appropriate*) . . . nowhere near Christmas.
C	Well cut off my legs and call me Shorty!
Boss	No I'm not very good at amputations. In any case, I had a dog once called Shorty. It died in a tumble drier. (*Makes as if to weep*)
C	OK. What's the score?
Boss	I want you to go out and spot elephants.
C	Do you mean infect them with measles?
Boss	No, I mean just spot them, count them, tally them up.
C	Do I need qualifications?
Boss	What have you got?
C	A GCSE in home economics. Oh, and a cycling proficiency badge.
Boss	Hmm . . . all right, I'll take you on.
C	When do I start?
Boss	Now.
C	When do I finish?
Boss	At 6 o'clock when I wave a packet of jelly babies at you.
C	Jelly babies!?
Boss	What's wrong, are you allergic to them?
C	No . . . (*Mocking the Boss*) It's just that I had a dog once which ate jelly babies.
Boss	And what happened to it?
C	It jumped into a tumble drier.
Boss	Go on!! (*C goes off, imitating a dog. Winds on clock to 3 and makes signs so as to waken D*) Do you . . .
D	(*Interjecting*) Its OK, I've heard it . . . spot the elephants. . . come back at six . . . packet of jelly babies as above . . . Bob's your auntie!
Boss	No, my auntie's name is Freda.
D	Has she had a sex change?
Boss	Look . . . you go and spot elephants . . . And I'd better think about phoning my auntie. (*D goes off*)
Boss	(*Winding clock to 5*) Wakey, wakey!
E	Hey, what's the time?
Boss	5 o'clock.
E	a.m. or p.m.?
Boss	Take your pick. If you think it's a.m., I'll give you 13 hours work. If you think it is p.m., I'll give you one hour's.

E	Oh, I'm just half-awake. You'd better make it p.m.
Boss	Right, off you go and join the others. They're just outside.
E	What are they doing?
Boss	Spotting elephants.
E	Are they 'all right'?
Boss	The elephants? Oh, I reckon so . . . Are you?
E	An elephant? No! The nearest think I get to a trunk is when I pack for holiday.
Boss	Out you go!
	(*E goes off. After a pause, the* Boss *goes to the door and blows a whistle. The five workers then return*)
All	(*Singing*) Ho hum, ho hum,
	its back from spotting elephants we come
	if you think that's a laugh,
	try to spot a giraffe
	ho hum, ho hum etc.
Boss	Thank you, thank you. Thank you for a day's work well done. Lets see though . . . how many have you spotted? You (*To A*) How many?
A	(*Tallying up on fingers*) Eh . . . none.
Boss	Very good. Now (*To B*), what about you?
B	None.
Boss	(*To C*) And you?
C	None.
Boss	(*To D*) And you?
D	None.
Boss	(*To E*) And you?
E	27 (*All look round in astonishment*)
Boss	27!?
E	No, I was only joking. I never saw any.
Boss	Well, here's your reward . . . your pay . . . your recompense . . . your quelquechose . . . your 'je ne sais pas'.
E	A funny name for jelly babies! (*Boss gives them a packet each*)
D	(*Annoyed*) Hey, wait a minute!
Boss	Yes?
D	How come I was out there for three hours elephant spotting and he gets the same as me, and he was only out for fifty-five minutes?
C	And how come I was out for six hours elephant spotting and he (*D*) gets the same as me and he (*E*) gets the same as me?

26

B	How come I was out for nine hours and I get the same as he (C) got, and he (D) got, and he (E) got?
A	How come I've been out since 6 o'clock this morning, and I get the same as him (B) and him (C) and him (D) and him (E)?
E	(*As aggressively as A at first, then quietening down*) Yes ... and how come I was out there for fifty-five minutes . . . and I get . . . eh . . . and I get . . . the same as . . . him and . . .
A	(*To Boss, interrupting E*) Right, come clean! This is not fair! It's not fair, and it's not just!
Boss	Just? . . . Oh yes, it is just . . . by my standards. And you . . . you are jealous because I am kind . . . Jealous because I believe that the first shall be last and the least is as important as the greatest?
A	Wait a minute . . . you're beginning to sound just like Jesus!
Boss	Lets go and spot some more elephants and we'll talk about it.

John Bell and Graham Maule

Reading   Matthew 20.1-16

Reflection   *Expand on the following comment.*
God does not balance our behaviour with his love like the scales of justice. God is generous in giving us what we need and not what we deserve.

Hymn   'O Lord, all the world belongs to you'

Prayers of Intercession
Divide into small informal groups, preferably of mixed ages. Invite each group to think about the 'turning the world upside down' theme and read the Magnificat towards the beginning of worship. What in our lives, in the church and in the world needs turning upside down? Reflect on a God who meets our need instead of giving us what we deserve. What in fact do we, the church and the world need?

After a short time, stop the discussions. Ask everyone to be quiet and think about what has been said and then to offer their thoughts to God. Conclude with the following prayer.

Prayer
Lord, amaze us again in your love by giving us and your whole creation what we need rather than what we deserve. Turn our

thinking and our living upside down so that our living and the life of the world may show the signs of your kingdom. Lead us from justice to love, and then fill our love with delight.   Amen

Hymn   'The kingdom of God is justice and joy'

Benediction

TRUE MEMORIALS
A service for Remembrance Sunday

Introduction

Many people, including those who lead worship find difficulty with Remembrance Sunday. Two World Wars are being remembered and in spite of the fact that war has been ever present in the world since 1945 and has been brought into our homes via television and radio, most of us do not share the personal memories of those who lived or served through a World War. What then can war memorials or 'remembrance' mean to most people in British society who are too young to remember either 1914–1918 or 1939–1945?

This service, therefore, approaches Remembrance Sunday through the idea that behind every 'memorial' there is a story which can inspire people to create their own future. Memorials are not only about the past; they are about the future!

The custom of the local church for the observance of Remembrance Sunday can be included at the start of the service or at 11.00 a.m. as desired.

Preparation

Learn to sing 'Dona nobis pacem'. The words and music are given on page 35.

Cut out headlines from the week's news. Arrange for them to be held up and read out in the service. Alternatively, photocopy them onto an overhead projector acetate ready to project.

ORDER OF WORSHIP

Opening Sentence

The God of peace be with you all. Amen

Romans 15.33

Prayer

Almighty God, you inspire the hearts and minds of all your people. May we always love to do what you command.

29

May your peace be our peace; may it live in our hearts and flow out in our lives.
As your love brings us together, may we understand your purpose for life and work, and live it, so that peace will cover the earth. To the glory of Jesus Christ our Lord. Amen

Hymn   'Lord, for the years your love has kept and guided'
              or 'Thy hand, O God, has guided'

Reading

Remember Ypres, the Somme, Mons and Verdun.
Remember the Western Desert, El Alamein, the Normandy beaches.
Remember Dresden, Hiroshima and the Burma Road.
Remember Korea, the Falkland Islands and Northern Ireland.

Remember the courage, the comradeship, the ingenuity,
the spirit of working together for a common cause,
the planning together for a better world
that would come with peace.

Remember the call to arms, the patriotic songs, the posters,
the partings which were such sweet sorrow,
the sound of the drum, the skirl of the pipe,
the prayer that God would be on our side.

Remember the carnage;
the colossal, stinking, bloody horror;
the ripped bodies on the wire,
the platoons of which only three out of forty lived.
Remember the widows of sixty years and more,
the old men and women living now who never knew their fathers.
Remember the love that was lost, the wisdom wasted,
the minds that were twisted and the limbs distorted.

Remember the wealth of nations being fired from guns,
dropped as bombs:
smashing schools, homes, factories, churches and hospitals;
ruining crops, destroying trees.
Remember the hope of a whole generation
left to evaporate in the sands of a desert
or sink for ever in the oceans of the world.

Remember this day the children who will die while the world spends its wealth on arms; the young who will have no work while others in their generation are trained to fight; the ambulances that will not come while we argue about how many troop carriers we need; the research into disease left neglected while brilliant minds are used to study more effective destruction.

Remember the one who asked us to remember him.

Graham Cook

Silence

Introduce the silence according to the needs of the congregation on Remembrance Sunday. End the silence with the following prayer inviting the congregation, or a small group of singers, to sing 'Dona nobis pacem' as a response to each section.

Prayer

Lord,
when we pray for peace,
show us again and again,
that there can be no peace
without the establishment of justice,
and the renewal of integrity.
    'Dona nobis pacem . . .'

When we are tempted to retreat
into sentimental peace of mind,
stir within us
the passion for justice which Amos had,
the social vision of Isaiah,
the international courage of Jeremiah,
and the personal responsibility of Hosea.
    'Dona nobis pacem . . .'

Then, Lord,
within the struggle
for righteousness and equality,
for wholeness and honesty,
come to us with special greeting
which you alone can provide,
dispelling our eternal fears,

cancelling our guilt,
refreshing our spirits:
the welcome, the peace of your son,
Jesus Christ,
our Risen Lord.
   'Dona nobis pacem . . .'

David Jenkins

Hymn   'For the healing of the nations'

Comments
Invite different people to read the following Comments. Adapt where necessary.

Comment 1 – *Memorials around us*
They say that every picture tells a story. You discover how true that is if you come across some old holiday pictures. As you look at each picture, you are reminded of what happened to you and the friends or family you were with. It almost recreates the experience. If we split up the word remember into re - member, we can see it has a meaning of putting together again. However, if you show those pictures to someone who wasn't with you on that holiday, the pictures are simply of beaches and scenery and people they don't know. If you're not part of the story, the pictures are boring!

Invite the congregation to look around the church building at any 'memorials' or reminders there are – plaques on the wall, photographs (of this year's outing as well as of ministers from earlier this century!), things given by people, cradle rolls, even the church building itself. Encourage members of the congregation to tell the story of what event or person each 'memorial' commemorates. Each 'memorial' reminds us of the story behind it.

Hymn   'God is love, his the care'

Comment 2 – *Memorials from the past*
'Have you ever visited Stonehenge? It's a very mysterious place. Huge pieces of rock planted on end in the ground. Some resting across the top of upright blocks. Almost everyone who goes there comes away with questions in their minds. Why was it built all those hundreds of years ago? How did people without heavy lorries and cranes manage to build it?' We would love to know the real story but

no one knows for sure. People have thought up all kinds of explanations.

Early in the Old Testament, we can read the story of Joshua. Moses led the Israelites out of slavery in Egypt but it was Joshua who took over the leadership for the last part of the journey into the promised land. It was a very important day when the Israelites crossed the River Jordan. Listen to the story: *Read Joshua 4.1-10*. The standing stones Joshua and his men put up weren't as big as Stonehenge. But they did make people ask questions each time they saw them. Why were they there? The answer was the story of how God had used Joshua to lead the people into the promised land. The important thing was not the stones but the story of which they reminded people.

Some memorials give the wrong message. We have seen statues pulled down in the former Soviet Union because people no longer believed in the story behind the memorial. The poem *Ozymandias* by Shelley gives us a similar picture of the memorial not living up to its message.

I met a traveller from an antique land
Who said: two vast and trunkless legs of stone
Stand in the desert. Near them on the sand,
Half sunk, a shatter'd visage lies, whose frown
And wrinkled lip and sneer of cold command
Tell that its sculptor well those passions read
Which yet survive stamped on these lifeless things,
The hand which mock'd them and the heart that fed;
And on the pedestal these words appear:
'My name is Ozymandias, king of kings:
Look on my works, ye Mighty and despair!'
Nothing beside remains. Round the decay
Of that colossal wreck, boundless and bare,
The lone and level sands stretch far away.

Hymn   'Christ is the world's light'

Comment 3 – *Living Memorials*
The best memorials are not wood or brick or stone or concrete, they are people.

War memorials don't tell the whole story of the freedoms people fought for but people and nations who live in freedom and peace do. Church buildings don't tell the whole story of Christian faith but people who try to follow in the way of Christ do. We are living memorials; people can look at us and be reminded of God and his love.

Jesus said 'Like the lamp, you must shed light among your fellows, so that, when they see the good you do, they may give praise to your Father in heaven.'

Matthew 5.16 (REB)

Prayers of Intercession
Use the headlines from newspapers of the last few days as biddings. Sing 'Dona nobis pacem' as a response to each. If a small group sang the response earlier in the service the congregation will have learnt the words and tunes and be able respond corporately.

Hymn 'This we can do for justice and for peace'
or 'Make me a channel of your love'

Concluding Prayer
Invite the congregation to say this together
Lord make us instruments of your peace.
Where there is hatred, let us sow love;
where there is injury, pardon;
where there is discord, union;
where there is doubt, faith;
where there is despair, hope;
where there is darkness, light;
where there is sadness, joy;
for your mercy and your truth's sake. Amen.

Francis of Assisi

Benediction

Dona nobis pacem (Anon)

Do - na no - bis pa - cem, pa - cem;

do - na no - bis pa - cem.

Do - na no - bis pa - cem,

do - na no - bis pa - cem.

Do - na no - bis pa - cem,

do - na no - bis pa - cem.

Grant us peace.

ACKNOWLEDGEMENTS

The editor and publishers gratefully acknowledge permission to reproduce the following copyright material.

Every effort has been made to trace copyright owners but if any rights have been inadvertently overlooked, the necessary correction will be made in subsequent editions. We apologise for any apparent negligence.

David Cowling:
   From *Sixty Second Thoughts*, edited by Jonathan Kerry used by
   permission of Methodist Church Division of Education & Youth.
Janet Morley:
   From *ALL Desires Known*, (SPCK 1992) used by permission of the
   author.
John Bell & Graham Maule:
   The Jube Jube Man, from *Wild Goose Prints 1*, used by permission
   of the Iona Community 1985.
Graham Cook:
   Remember Ypres, from *Liturgy of Life* (NCEC), used by permission
   of the author.
David Jenkins:
   Lord When We Pray For Peace, from *Liturgy of Life* (NCEC), used
   by permission of the author.

We are grateful to quote from the following version of the Bible:
REB   *The Revised English Bible* (© 1989 Oxford and Cambridge
   University Presses).